A Matter Of The Heart

A collection of modern psalms

by Leah Guanipa

Let us find a good musician to play the lyre
whenever the distressing spirit troubles you.
He will play soothing music and you will soon be well again.

1 Samuel 16:16

A Matter Of The Heart is a collection of my original songs. Each song is an intimate glimpse of a conversation between my maker and I, inspired by dreams, visions and my personal walk with Christ. They are a poetic expression of love, hope, and truth using words and song.

As a child, I struggled with being profoundly timid and often felt withdrawn from the world, something I carried with me into adulthood. Writing these songs has been the healing salve that my soul needed; an affirmation of my true identity as an unconditionally loved child of God.

May they be a source of hope and healing for you as well.

-Leah

Table Of Contents

This Kind of Love

Let David play the golden lyre
to soothe the demons plaguing Saul
A wicked heart one pure desire...
the prophet warned his crown would fall

Anointed long before the Answer
Made for a purpose so divine
Forsake this world, do not romance her
You've got the angels on your side

I don't know, no I don't know, but I can trust
this kind of Love
No I can't see, no I can't feel, but I can trust
this kind of Love

No I don't claim to have the answers
But I can offer you the Truth
If you don't have the Holy Spirit...
There's no life inside of you

I will sing unto the Angels
Unto the Lion and the Lamb
No, I don't live to please the people
because I know who I am

No, I don't live to please the people
Because I know who I am!

I don't know, no I don't know, but I can trust
this kind of Love
No I can't see, no I can't feel, but I can trust
this kind of Love

I don't want this life, don't want this world
I just want your love

No I don't want this life, don't want this world

I just want...this kind of Love

I'm with You

What's your story?
Where are you?
You can speak
I will listen
Not accuse

Life ain't easy
That I know is true
Just remember this…
this one important truth

I'm with you

Sweet like honey
My words seep through
And these afflictions
Well I've…
I've carried them too

So take my burden
It's lighter for you
And just remember this…
this one important truth

I'm with you

Though your journey may feel long
You are right where you belong
Though you feel you can't go on
Don't you worry, I am strong

I am strong

So what's your story…?
Where are you…?
You can speak
I will listen
Not accuse

Life ain't easy
That I know is true
Just remember this…
this one important truth

I'm with you

The Dream

I had another dream last night
A different world though a beautiful sight
It did not contain pain or sin
The kind of place thy good saint would be in

With golden castles
And a throne for a king
A beautiful sunset and angels that sing

Angels that sing

My eyes now open and reality is here
I now see pain and sin and fear
I wish I could go back to my dream domain
It's different from this world, it's hard to explain

With Golden castles
A throne for a king
A beautiful sunset and angels that sing

Angels that sing

A place that's worthy
Sincere and true
Not vile not filthy
One I wish to pursue

One I wish to pursue

In the Spring

Every book has a voice
has a meaning
and when I read
I see what you're seeing

Because you've recommended this book for me…
and now I have your golden key
your key, your key
And now I have your golden key

If I pick a flower
in an empty field
I know right away
that my heart has been healed

'Cuz when I get home I see…
that the rest have been picked for me

And when our souls are tied together
they're strong as a fist yet light as a feather
Oh everywhere we go there's spring no snow
no harsh winds, and the water flows

Oh everywhere we go
there's spring no snow no harsh winds
and the water flows… in the spring

In the spring
Well baby, maybe… in the spring

Let me see what I can reveal
about our love, with a kiss it is sealed
I never knew what you thought of me
but now I have your memories, of me
of me…oh now I have your memories

Oh, everybody please sing it with me
How much better this day can get
We're so happy. Happy. Happy.
How much better this day can get we're so happy!

And when our souls are tied together
they're strong as a fist yet light as a feather
Oh everywhere we go there's spring no snow
no harsh winds, and the water flows

Oh everywhere we go
there's spring no snow no harsh winds
and the water flows in the spring
In the spring…

Well baby, maybe, in the spring
In the spring, in the spring
Well maybe, baby… in the spring

Small Fish

When your no longer
a big fish in the pond
but a small fish
in the ocean that goes beyond

You may stumble
You may fall
But don't you dare get on your knees and crawl
Because it's your time
So stand up nice and tall

I won't always be there to
hold your hand, baby
I'm going to need you to
say "yes I can..."

I won't always be there to
break your fall, baby
I'm going to need you to
stand up nice and tall

There will be many
challenges to take
So encounter them boldly
Try not to make mistakes

You may stumble
You may fall
But don't you dare get on your knees and crawl
Because it's your time
So stand up nice and tall

I won't always be there to
hold your hand, baby
I'm going to need you to
say "yes I can"

I won't always be there to
break your fall, baby
I'm going to need you to
stand up nice and tall

It's your time

Listen up

Listen up to this song I sing to you today
A melody, a symphony, of love
I will sing it not once, not twice
but seven times, with eleven rhymes
to please the wonderous man above

It seems like everywhere I go,
there's always people, places to know
Life is not one big puzzle, 'tis a journey
So take that right path
as wisdom calls throughout the streets
Don't let ignorance or prideness get in the way

So I ask you, my dear please
to listen up to this melody, this symphony of love
Of love...
I will sing it not once, not twice
but seven times, with eleven rhymes
to please the wonderous man above

He's Coming Home

No I don't belong here, this isn't my home
You don't know my Father, He sits on His throne
My kingdom's not from here, it comes from above
And this crown that I wear
I wear it with Love

Because I know
Yes I know
He's coming home

My body is dying, my soul's still alive
My spirit is strong, so I know I'll survive
I know it's not easy, this fight in your mind
The cares of this world, just leave them behind

Because I know
Yes I know
He's coming home

To Be Alive

Words…they bring death or they bring life
It's in the tongue our power resides
It may take the renewing of your mind
That divine perspective is a one of a kind

So I…I was sent to open your mind
So you, you can go and live your lives
To hear, this truth before ends time

To Be Alive is to Live in Christ

Wake up! From this sleep and open your eyes
He'll come like a thief in the middle of the night
I speak the truth, I tell no lies
So hear these words, this sweet lullaby

To Be Alive is to Live in Christ

To Be Alive is to Live in Christ

Written on Your Palm

I was written on your palm
then created all day long
For you I'll wait
and I'll sing my songs
Because in this world
I know I don't belong

I will set my eyes above
For there lies my treasure
there lies my Love
For you I'll gladly sacrifice
For you I'll give up my own life

For you I'll give up my own life

You know every thought that I have
You know when I'm happy
when I'm sad
And every hair you've counted on my head
For me you've died, your blood you have shed

I will set my eyes above
For there lies my treasure
there lies my Love
For you I'll gladly sacrifice
For you I'll give up my own life

For you I'll give up my own life

Secret Place

Won't you take me to that
secret place
I want to feed my soul

I am thirsty just to
see your face
before I grow old

Won't you?

I watch the children as they
laugh and play
I remember when I was told...

time goes by like it was
yesterday
I see the truth unfold

Won't you?

Won't you take me to that
secret place
I want to feed my soul

I am thirsty just to
see your face
before I grow old

Won't you...?

A Matter of the Heart

Would you give it all up for me
Unlock your heart and hand me the key
Would you trust me with your very life
Hand me your vision, I'll give you my sight

Would you think of me every morning
Would you dream of me every night
Would you make me your one and only
Make that body and soul sacrifice

It's a matter of the heart

You know that I've written a book about you
I hope you read it, I pray it comes true
And all of your days were already ordained
For you I've been waiting in that secret place

Would you think of me every morning
Would you dream of me every night
Would you make me your one and only
Make that body and soul sacrifice

It's a matter of the heart

For you've I've been waiting, all my life
I will meet you, in paradise
I will see you, when I die

Mockingbird

Mockingbird don't mock me
No repeating words of mine, words of mine
I sing them just fine, I sing them just fine

And if I make a small, tedious mistake
please don't repeat me, for Heaven's sake

Because I know
what you long for
each and every day
It's to hear
the sound of music
and to mimic what it says

Let me hear your own song
Sing to me today
Write lyrics I haven't heard
Ones no one else would say

Let me hear your sweet voice
The one that comes from heart
Play thy only melody
So I don't fall apart

And you'll see…
That you'll be free

If a crow comes around
don't be afraid
to sing too loud, to sing too loud
You need to make that voice of yours
an echoing sound, an echoing sound

And if that crow says to stop
when the sun…
the sun comes down, the sun comes down
You need to say no, no
this is my sound, this is my sound

Because I know
what you long for
each and every day
It's to hear
the sound of music
and to mimic what it says

Let me hear your own song
Sing to me today
Write lyrics I haven't heard
Ones no one else would say

Let me hear your sweet voice
The one that comes from heart
Play thy only melody
So I don't fall apart

And you'll see…
That you'll be free

Song of Solomon

You are more than I thought I ever wanted
Oh your love is far sweeter than wine
Oh my King won't you take me to your palace?
And maybe meet me in the garden tonight

And when I see you, I feel like I could die
You are my hearts desire, you set my soul fire

Did you not know you're the Lily of the valley?
Your like a rose among the others, they are thorns
And your eyes like a dove you look my way
I'm overcome by the beauty you adorn

And when I see you, I feel like I could die
You are my hearts desire, you set my soul fire

And when I touch you, I feel like I'm alive
Oh for you I've waited, I've waited all my life

Yes for you I've waited, I've waited all my life

To the Ends of the Earth

I am one with you in spirit
You are hidden in my soul
I will dance with you, 'til the end of time
A love this world has never known

I will sit with you in Heaven
Ruling right beside your throne
I will wear this crown
Put on this pretty gown
Revealing mysteries unknown

My life was never mine
Inside this grand design
The world is yours
And yours alone

I will follow you...to the ends of the earth

Always living in the moment
Learning all there is to learn
I may laugh or cry
Say my hellos, goodbyes
Watching as the world is turning

No, I don't care about the money
I could care less for the fame
As time is fleeting I...
Grow older and more wise
I've come to learn it's all in vain

So I won't waste my time
No I won't compromise
It's death we all cannot escape

So I will follow you...to the ends of the earth

A mortal in this world, not of it
How my heart longs for your return
Well I am free and wild
With faith that of a child
A soul this world does not concern

I will dance with you
'Til the end of time
A love this world has never known

So I will follow you
I will follow you
I will follow you

...To the ends of the earth

Look What I'm Doing

Can you not see it?
Do you not perceive it?
This new thing I'm doing through you
The old has gone, the new has come
Look what I'm doing to you!

All of your days, were never a waste
No, your suffering wasn't in vain
So take my hand, and take a stand
and claim my promises today

I will give back to you, all that was stolen
You once had it all, until after the fall
I will redeem you, clean you up and restore you
I will free you from all, your new name I will call

I will call you by your name
The name I called you before you were born
I saw you when you were formed,
inside your mothers womb

Look what I'm doing!
Look what I'm doing through you!

Live Forever

I saw a man, down by the water
You wouldn't believe, what he had to offer
He knew about me, my past and my present,
my whole family, and all my descendants

He said "Do you want to live forever?
Do you want to come with me? Come and drink
this living water, come with me and you shall see."

He said unto me, "Tell the whole world,"
"What I have to give, is more than jewels and pearls."
He said "I give life and freedom from sin.
And your world cannot offer, this peace that I bring."

And if they don't believe, and their eyes cannot see
they will reject you, so fulfill prophecy.

Do you want to live forever?
Do you want to come with me? Come and drink
this living water, come with me and you shall see.

Do you want to live forever? Do you want your
life to change? Come and drink this living water!
You will never be the same!

Chosen

I've got no fancy message for you
Just my voice and these guitar strings too
I will make sure to empty my body
like a vessel for Him to flow through

Like a vessel for Him to flow through

And you...
chose the weak and the foolish
chose the ones that the world has rejected...
to shine your light through

And I...
find there's so much more meaning
find there's so much more purpose in life...
when I'm living for you

How come I feel I never fit in
When I try, I just can't seem to win
Now I know I was made for much greater
Something special inside me within

Something special inside me within

And you...
chose the weak and the foolish
chose the ones that the world has rejected...
to shine your light through

And I...
find there's so much more meaning
find there's so much more purpose in life...
when I'm singing for you

So don't...
don't be discouraged
if they all hate you just know
that they first hated me

So sing!
Sing for my people!
Show them the meaning of life
and set their minds free

And you!
You are not of this world...
You will never fit in...

You were chosen

If It Saves My Soul

Like a city with its walls down
is when I had no self control
I will surely fight this good fight
if it means it'll save my soul

When the spirit fell upon me
so white and pure like a dove
I will leave this world behind me
and store my treasures up above

To truly live…I must give up my life
Feed my spirit and my flesh I sacrifice

To feel alive…I myself must die
To truly live…I must give up my own life

If it means it'll save my soul…

Made in the Image

I want to know you
I want to touch your face
I've heard you've many names...
of which one is grace

The world thinks I'm foolish
for the way that I speak of you
But I don't seem to care...
you're the only thing that's true

And I don't know what I would do...
if I can't live life with you

Flesh of my flesh
Bone of my bone, it's true
You're the air that I breathe
No, my heart cannot beat without you

I'm the dust of the earth
I was built from the ground, I'm new
Yes, I'm made in the image
I'm made in the image of you

I want to hear you
I want to sing your words
I've got so many desires...
but I choose to put you first

All of these symphonies,
these melodies, these works of art
They all don't mean anything...
if you don't play a part

And I don't know what I would do...
if I can't live life with you

Yes I'm made in the image...
I'm made in the image of you

It Shall Come

When I speak…
there are rubies, there are diamonds
there is treasure…
flowing from my tongue

When I hear…
when I listen, when I open my mind…
my body feels so young

And I know, yes I know
there are blessings
there are curses
and whatever you so utter shall be done

Yes I know, yes I know
I'm a daughter, I'm a princess…
of the Kingdom of Zion it's to come

It shall come

When I hide
I take shelter, in the shadow
of the Almighty El Shaddai

You're my strength
you're my alter, you're my stronghold
For you I choose to live…
only to die

And I know, yes I know
It's my calling, my anointing
to set your people free
with my songs

And yes I know, yes I know
an awakening, a revival
The day their eyes soon open…
won't be long

It shall come

The Vision

Hear your people shout with glory
Hear your people shout with joy

And all your sons and daughter will...
will prophesy
And all the old men will dream dreams...
dreams in the night

So write down that vision
And run, run with it
It will not tarry it will come
Just wait for it
Wait for it

Wait for it

Hear your people shout with glory
Hear your people shout with joy

I will pray in spirit and words that I understand
When the whole world's burning
I know I'm safe in your hands
And this revelation I can trust, will come to pass
And these tribulations I know, they won't last

So write down that vision
And run, run with it
It will not tarry it will come
Just wait for it...

Wait for it

The Words of my Father

These words that I've spoken
will come back fulfilled to me
Like a seed that was planted…
it shall grow up into a tree

And my heart confesses
that unto which I believe
these words that you've spoken
over me

Beauty for ashes
and a garment of praise
Today you shall give me
all this freedom that I crave

So take heart my darling
Things won't always be the same
And don't feel disheartened
There's still time to change your ways

And don't feel discouraged
as we near to these last days

But the words of my Father…
they remain

And these words that I've spoken
shall come back fulfilled to me
And the words of my Father
shall go down in history
And the words you declare
shall fulfill your destiny

It's these words that I've spoken
It's these words that I've sung
It's these words that I've spoken…

Over me

Child of Light

Darkness can't comprehend the light
No demon can understand the story of his life
No, I won't be dancing with my shadow
Because I know that I'm a child of light

I understand all the things of the spirit
And it bothers and baffles the men of this world
I come and I go like the wind, you can't see me
Like the ocean I'm full of treasure, full of gold

I've got all I need because you placed it deep inside me
So I humbly bow down, and wait for your return

No, I won't be dancing with my shadow
Because I know that I'm a child of light

Yes I know that I'm a child...
A child of light.

The Life is in the Blood

I was there when the oceans were formed
and your Spirit hovered over the waters
I was there when the sun and the moon
and the stars were written in the Heavens

No, you can't stop this melody deep in my heart
You can't stop the Angels from songs they impart
And whenever I pray, I always get what I ask for

Because the life is in the blood
Yes, the life is in the blood

I'll be there when your hair's white as snow
and your eyes, they flicker flames of fire
I'll be there when the sword's in your hand
and it's double-bladed with power

No, you can't stop this melody deep in my heart
You can't stop the Angels from songs they impart
And whenever I pray, I always get what I ask for

Because the life is in the blood
Yes, the life is in the blood

In the Blood

City of David

Hold on to that vision
Take care of that dream
Don't judge the future
based on what you can see

Your own ears will hear Him
a voice from behind
He will direct you
to the left or the right

In the City of David
Sustaining my dreams
You're a place full of worship
With a hope and a means

You're the Kingdom of Zion
My Jerusalem
You are carefully hidden
But revealed to some

You're the City of David

When you're weary and tired
You've done all you can do
Oh let go of your worries
Let that dream carry you

Don't stop believing
in the truth of His life
No, the world won't stop fighting you
But they can't stop your light

In the City of David
Sustaining my dreams
You're a place full of worship
With a hope and a means

You're the Kingdom of Zion
My Jerusalem
You are carefully hidden
But revealed to some

You're the City of David

Alpha Omega

I saw a light that covered all shadow
I said "What kind of light could that be?"
Then I saw it was the Holy Spirit
making its way through me

You will see
it's no fantasy
no fantasy
it is greater than can be
it is He

It is He

Alpha Omega
Beginning and End

In the beginning
when your prophecy came true
your story became known
but some did not believe you

You will see
it's no fantasy
no fantasy
it is greater than can be
it is He

It is He

Alpha Omega
Beginning and End

A Song to be Remembered

You will be remembered
A song of your own
But what is it worth
to gain the whole world
and lose your very own soul?

You could have all the knowledge
All the riches in the world
But if you have not Love, if you have not Love
You have nothing, nothing at all

This song lives forever
This message of mine
Because my melody's sweet
My words all unique
And it stands the test of time

Oh I will be remembered
If I answer the call
But if I have not Love, if I have not Love
I have nothing, nothing at all

Oh you will be remembered
If it takes my last breath
Because you saved the whole world
You died for my soul
And you gave me life after death

If I have not Love, if I have not Love
I have nothing, nothing at all

A Matter of the Heart

Leah Guanipa

Words & Music by Leah Guanipa

G6 G G7 G6 Am
mor- ning? Would you
Am Fmaj7 G6
dream of me ev- ery night?
C C G G
Would you make me your one and on- ly?
G7 G6 Am Am
Make that bo- dy and soul sac- ri-
C Chorus
Fmaj7 G6 C C
fi- ce It's a ma- tter of the heart
Cadd11 C G G
It's a matt- er of the he-
Am C/A Fmaj7/A Asus2 Fmaj7
a- rt

A Verse
You know that I've wri- tten a book abo -ut
G6 Am Am
you
Fmaj7 G6 Am
And I hope you
read it I pray it comes t- r- u- e
Am Fmaj7 G6
And all of your days were al- rea- dy or- dained
Am Am Fmaj7
For you I've been wait- ing in that sec- ret
G6 Am Am
B Pre-Chorus
Fmaj7 G6 C
pl- a- c- e
Would you

think of me every- y mor- ning?
C G G
58 59 60
Would you dream of me every- y ni- ght?
Am Am Fmaj7
61 62 63
G6 C
64 65 66
Would you make me . your one and
Am
67 68 69
on- ly? Make that
70 71 72
bo- dy and soul sac- ri- fi- ce It's a ma- tter of the heart
C Chorus
C C Cadd11 C G G
73 74 75
G Am Am
76 77 78
It's a matt- er of the he- ar- t

D Bridge
Fmaj7 G6 Fmaj7
For you I've been
wait- ing All my L- i- f- e
G6 C G Am
I will meet you in pa- ra-
Fmaj7 G6 C G
d- i- se I will see you
Am Fmaj7 G6
when I die
C G Am Fmaj7 Fadd9
Gadd9 G6 C G Am
Fmaj7 Fadd9 Gadd9 G6 C G

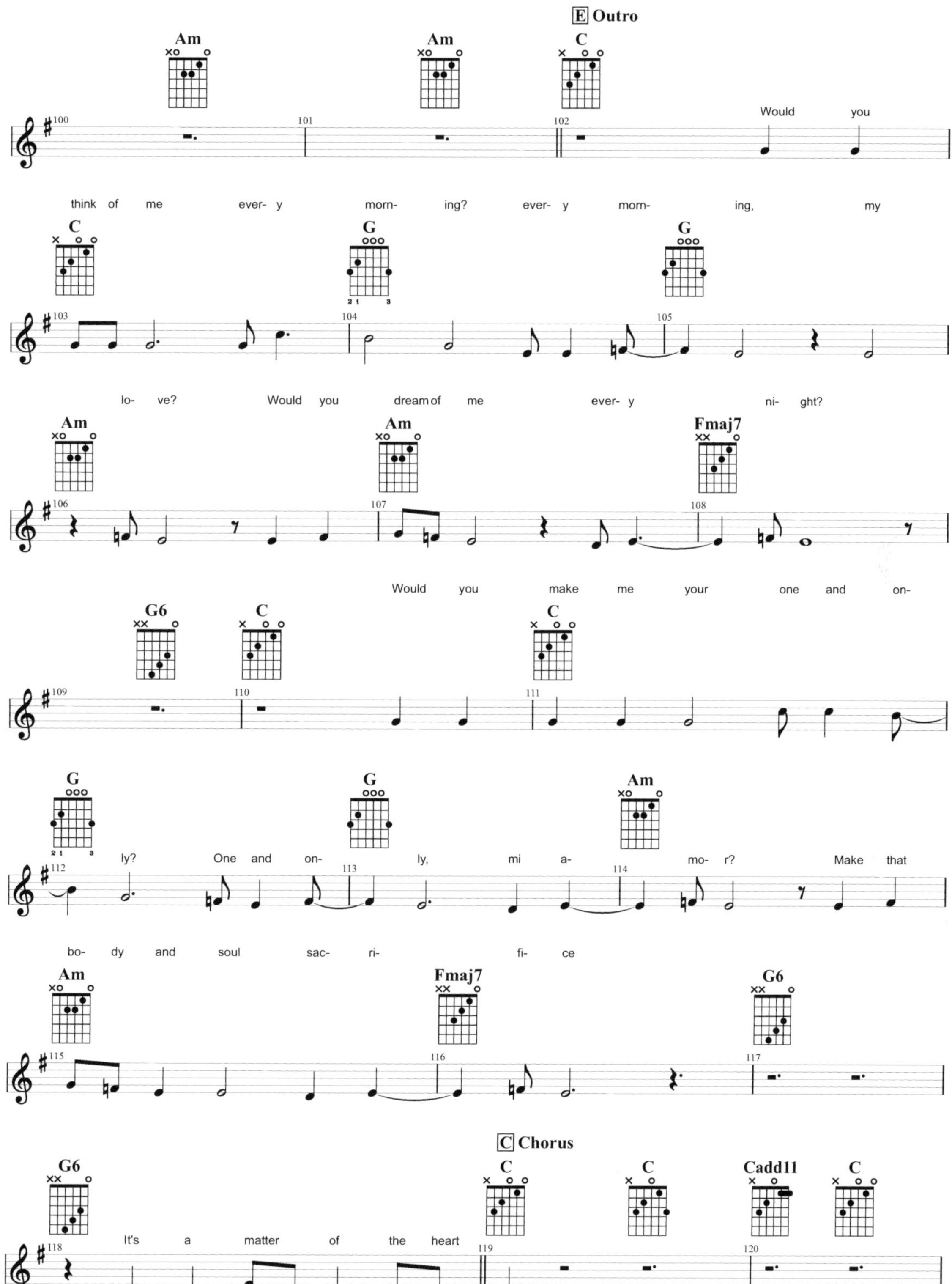
E Outro
Am Am C
Would you
think of me ever- y morn- ing? ever- y morn- ing, my
C G G
lo- ve? Would you dream of me ever- y ni- ght?
Am Am Fmaj7
Would you make me your one and on-
G6 C C
G G Am
ly? One and on- ly, mi a- mo- r? Make that
bo- dy and soul sac- ri- fi- ce
Am Fmaj7 G6
C Chorus
G6 C C Cadd11 C
It's a matter of the heart

G
G
Am
C/A
It's a matt- er of the he- ar- t
Asus2
Fmaj7
G6
G
C

Made in the USA
Columbia, SC
19 May 2024

35851757R00024